SCIENCE OF SPORTS

THE SCIENCE OF BASEBALL

WITH MAX AXIOM SUPER SCIENTIST

by David L. Dreier

illustrated by Maurizio Campidelli

Consultant:
Lyle A. Ford
Department Chair
Physics & Astronomy
University of Wisconsin, Eau Claire

CAPSTONE PRESS
a capstone imprint

Graphic Library is published by Capstone Press,
1710 Roe Crest Drive, North Mankato, Minnesota 56003
www.capstonepub.com

Library of Congress Cataloging-in-Publication Data
Drier, David.
  The science of baseball with Max Axiom, super scientist / by David Drier.
      pages cm.—(Graphic Library. The Science of Sports with Max Axiom.)
  Includes bibliographical references and index.
  Summary: "Uses graphic novel format to reveal the scientific aspects at play in the sport of
baseball"—Provided by publisher.
  ISBN 978-1-4914-6083-2 (library binding)
  ISBN 978-1-4914-6087-0 (paperback)
  ISBN 978-1-4914-6091-7 (eBook PDF)
  1. Baseball—Juvenile literature. 2. Sports sciences—Juvenile literature. 3. Graphic novels—
Juvenile literature. I. Title.
  GV867.5.D76 2016
  796.357—dc23   2015012514

Editor
Mandy Robbins

Designer
Ted Williams

Creative Director
Nathan Gassman

Cover Artist
Caio Cacau

Media Researcher
Jo Miller

Production Specialist
Laura Manthe

Printed in the United States of America in North Mankato, Minnesota.
042015   008823CGF15

TABLE OF CONTENTS

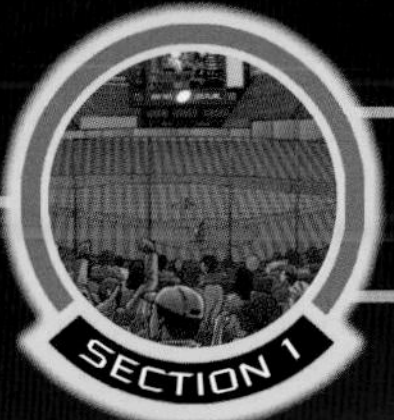
SECTION 1

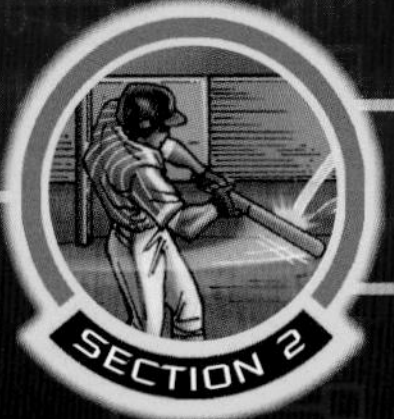
SECTION 2

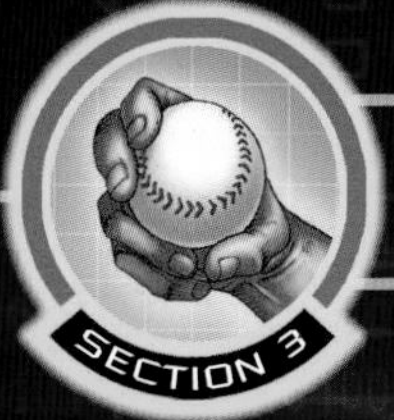
SECTION 3

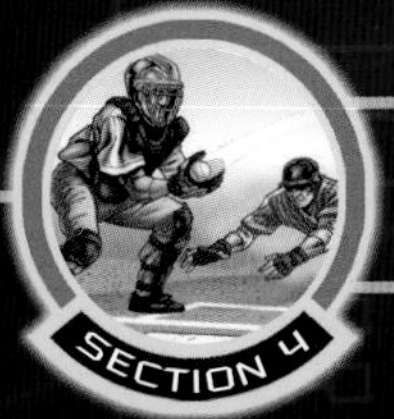
SECTION 4

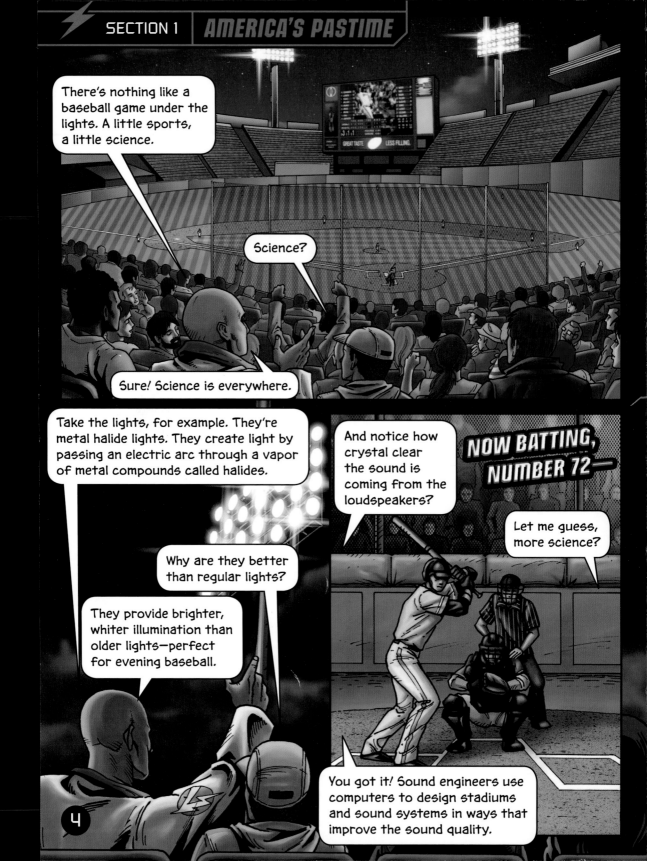

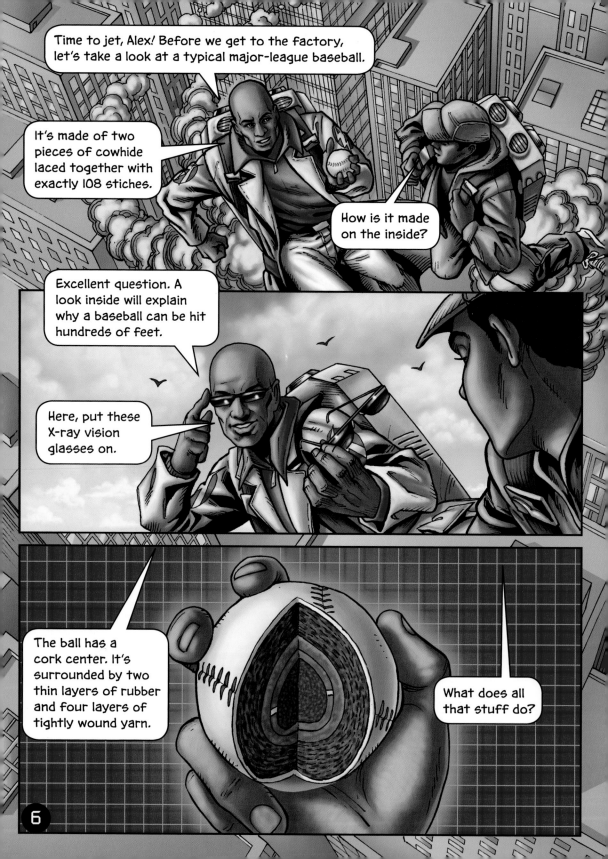

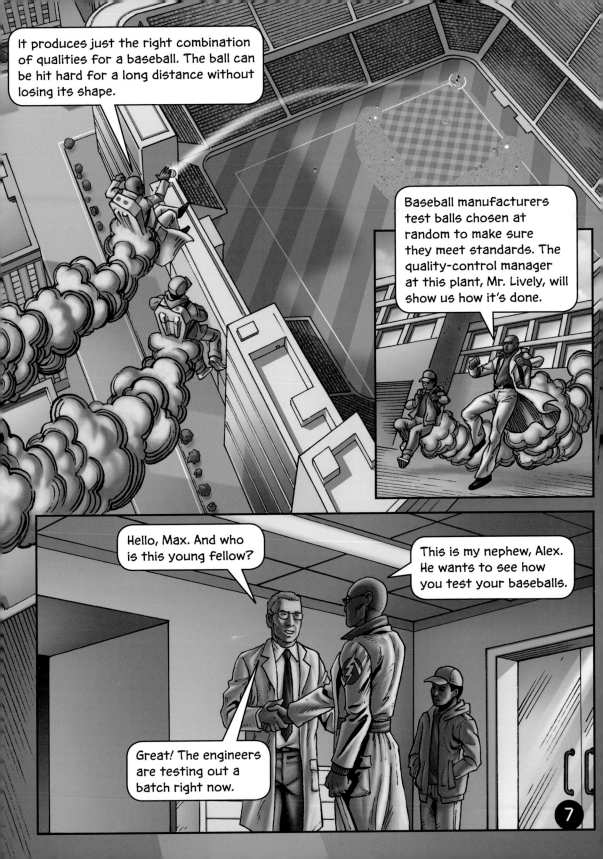

SECTION 2 | BATS AND HITTING

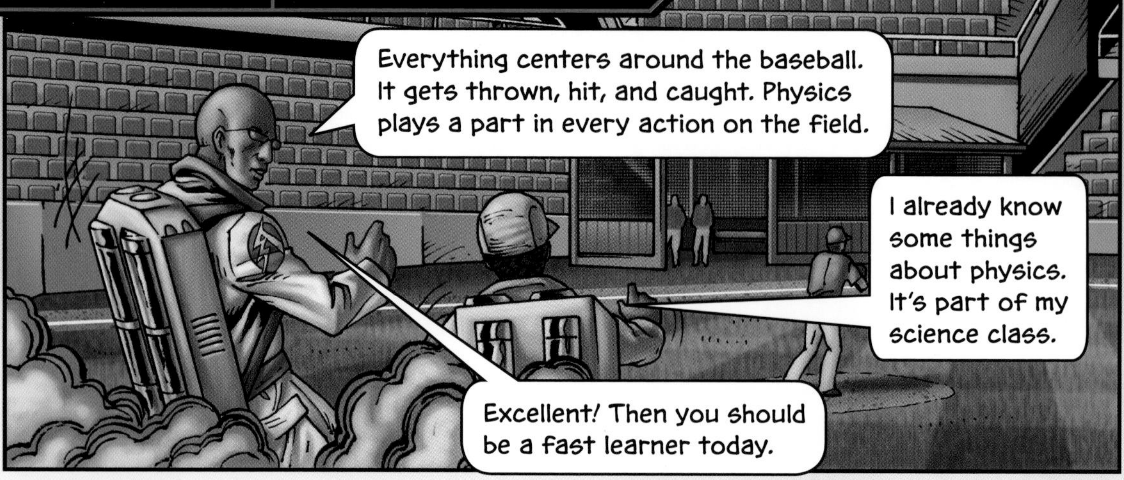
Everything centers around the baseball. It gets thrown, hit, and caught. Physics plays a part in every action on the field.
I already know some things about physics. It's part of my science class.
Excellent! Then you should be a fast learner today.

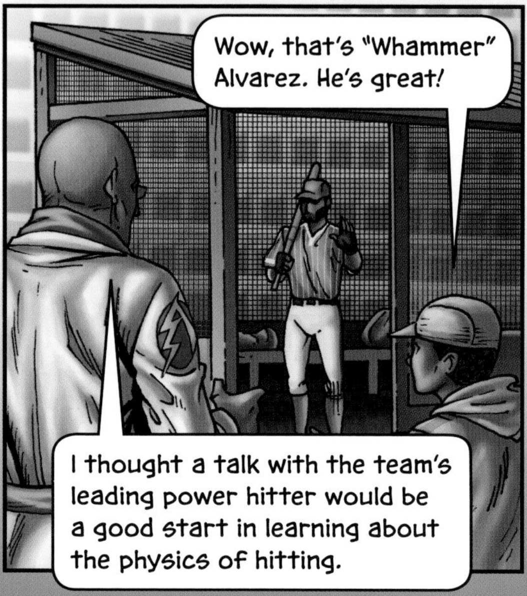
Wow, that's "Whammer" Alvarez. He's great!
I thought a talk with the team's leading power hitter would be a good start in learning about the physics of hitting.

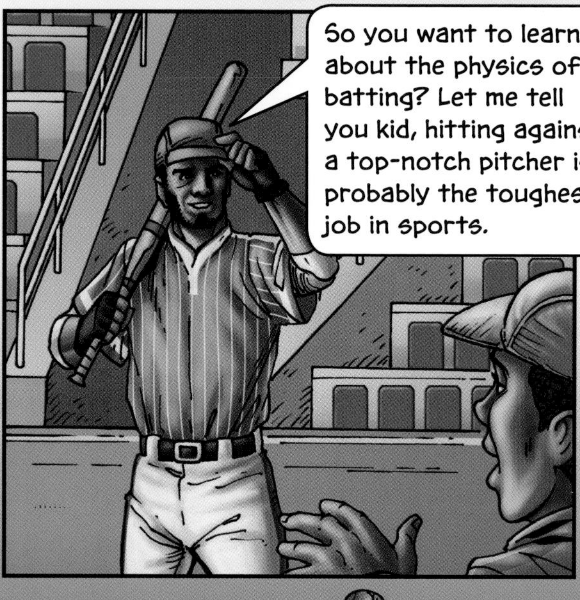
So you want to learn about the physics of batting? Let me tell you kid, hitting against a top-notch pitcher is probably the toughest job in sports.

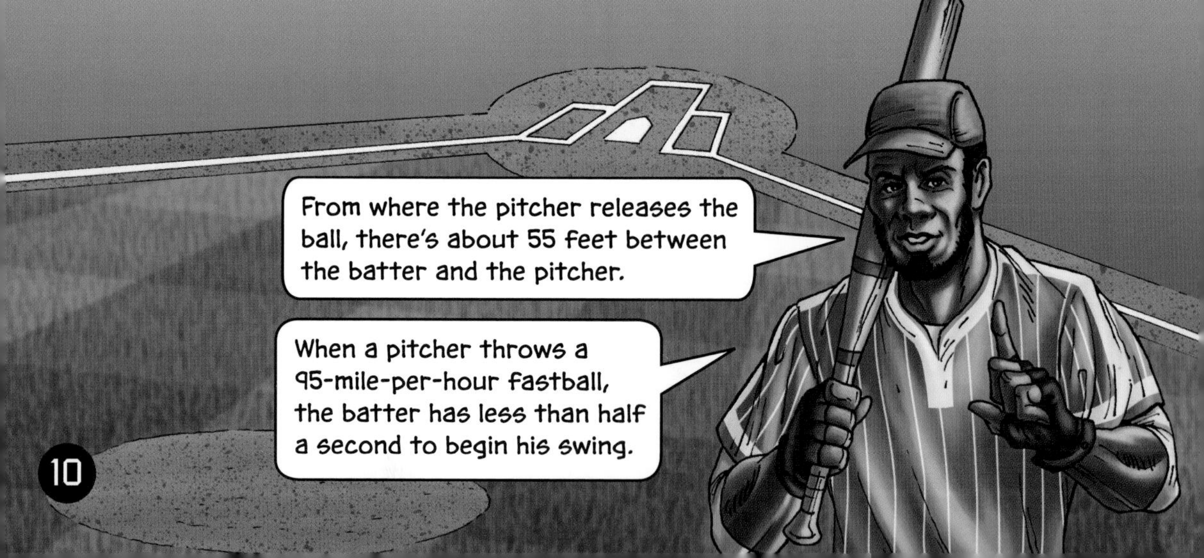
From where the pitcher releases the ball, there's about 55 feet between the batter and the pitcher.
When a pitcher throws a 95-mile-per-hour fastball, the batter has less than half a second to begin his swing.

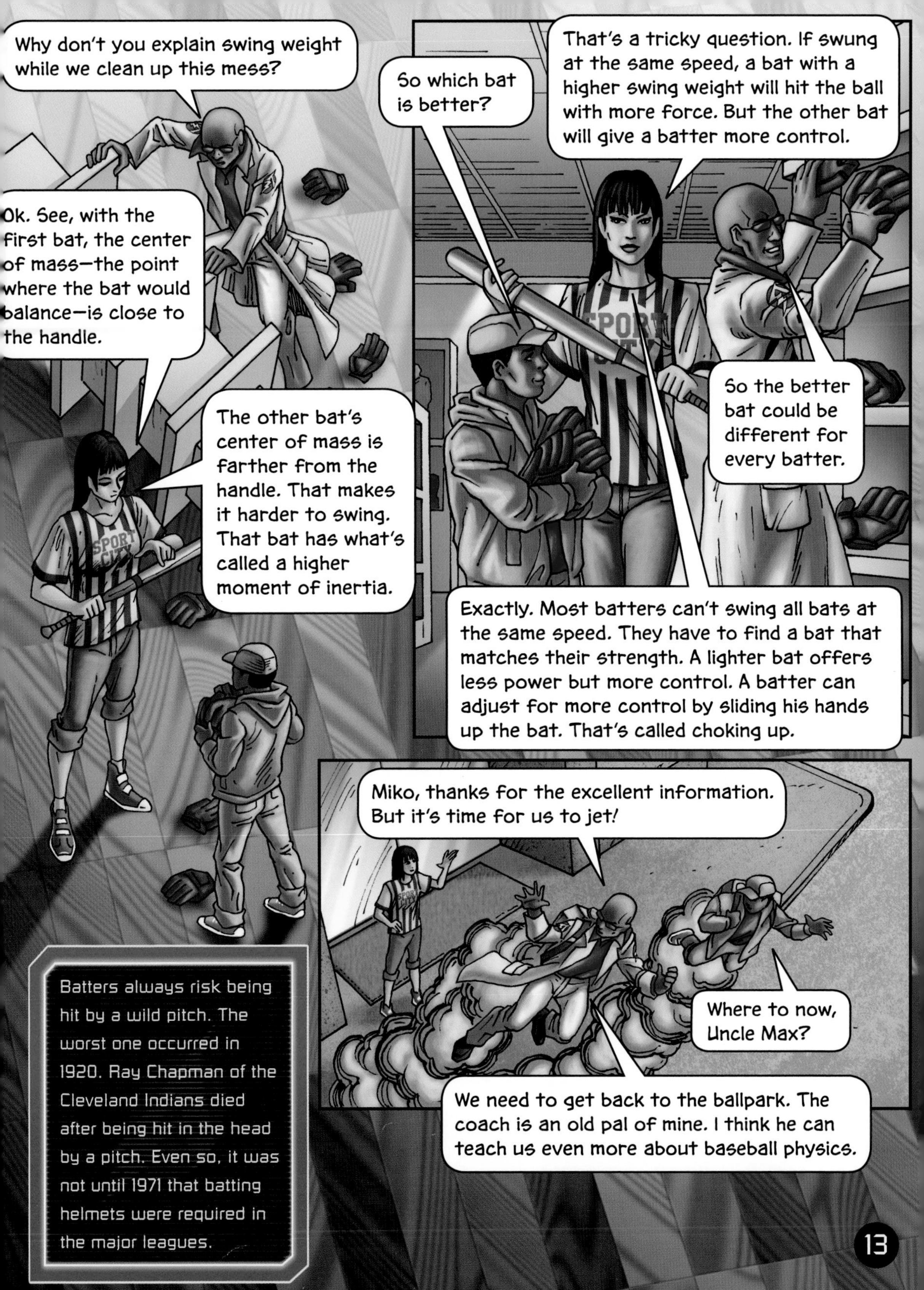
Why don't you explain swing weight while we clean up this mess?
Ok. See, with the first bat, the center of mass—the point where the bat would balance—is close to the handle.
The other bat's center of mass is farther from the handle. That makes it harder to swing. That bat has what's called a higher moment of inertia.
So which bat is better?
That's a tricky question. If swung at the same speed, a bat with a higher swing weight will hit the ball with more force. But the other bat will give a batter more control.
So the better bat could be different for every batter.
Exactly. Most batters can't swing all bats at the same speed. They have to find a bat that matches their strength. A lighter bat offers less power but more control. A batter can adjust for more control by sliding his hands up the bat. That's called choking up.
Batters always risk being hit by a wild pitch. The worst one occurred in 1920. Ray Chapman of the Cleveland Indians died after being hit in the head by a pitch. Even so, it was not until 1971 that batting helmets were required in the major leagues.
Miko, thanks for the excellent information. But it's time for us to jet!
Where to now, Uncle Max?
We need to get back to the ballpark. The coach is an old pal of mine. I think he can teach us even more about baseball physics.

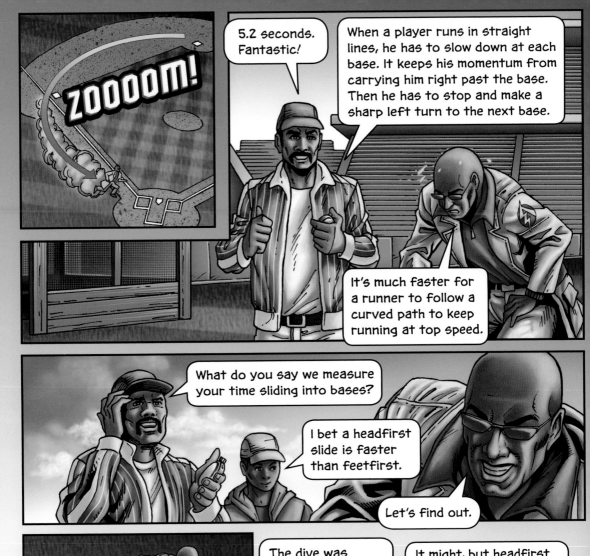

ZOOOOM!

5.2 seconds. Fantastic!

When a player runs in straight lines, he has to slow down at each base. It keeps his momentum from carrying him right past the base. Then he has to stop and make a sharp left turn to the next base.

It's much faster for a runner to follow a curved path to keep running at top speed.

What do you say we measure your time sliding into bases?

I bet a headfirst slide is faster than feetfirst.

Let's find out.

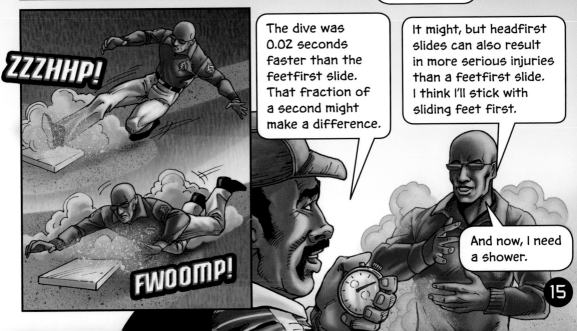

ZZZHHP!

The dive was 0.02 seconds faster than the feetfirst slide. That fraction of a second might make a difference.

It might, but headfirst slides can also result in more serious injuries than a feetfirst slide. I think I'll stick with sliding feet first.

And now, I need a shower.

FWOOMP!

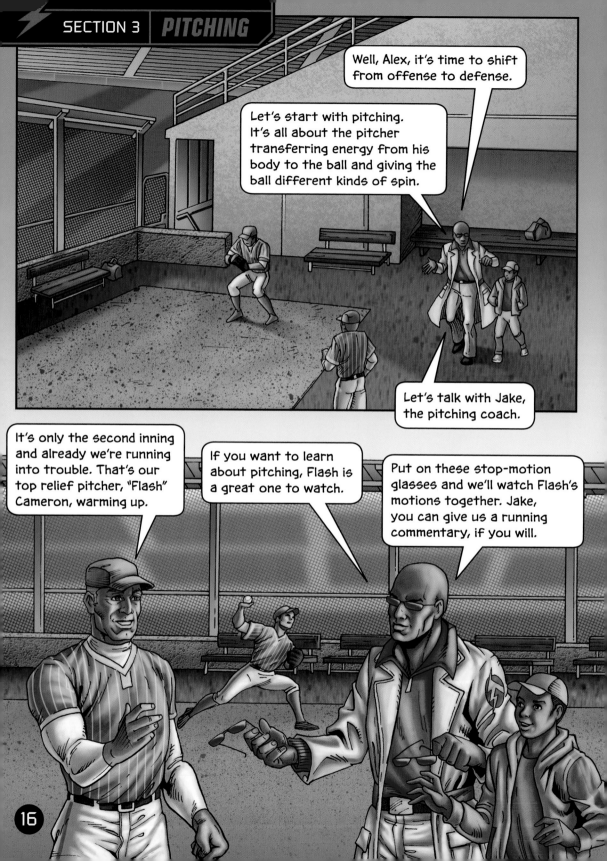

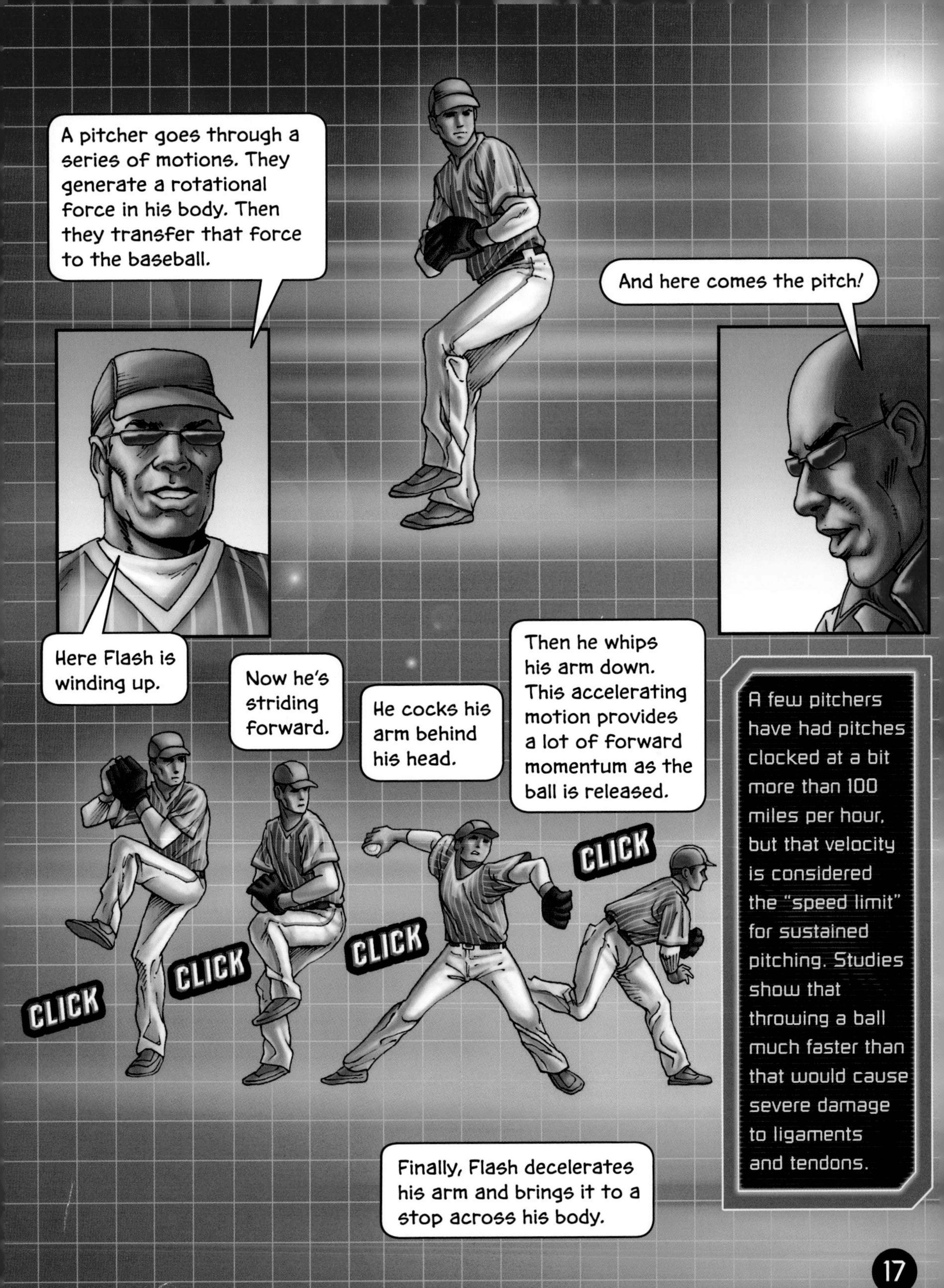
A pitcher goes through a series of motions. They generate a rotational force in his body. Then they transfer that force to the baseball.
And here comes the pitch!
Here Flash is winding up.
Now he's striding forward.
He cocks his arm behind his head.
Then he whips his arm down. This accelerating motion provides a lot of forward momentum as the ball is released.
A few pitchers have had pitches clocked at a bit more than 100 miles per hour, but that velocity is considered the "speed limit" for sustained pitching. Studies show that throwing a ball much faster than that would cause severe damage to ligaments and tendons.
CLICK
CLICK
CLICK
CLICK
Finally, Flash decelerates his arm and brings it to a stop across his body.

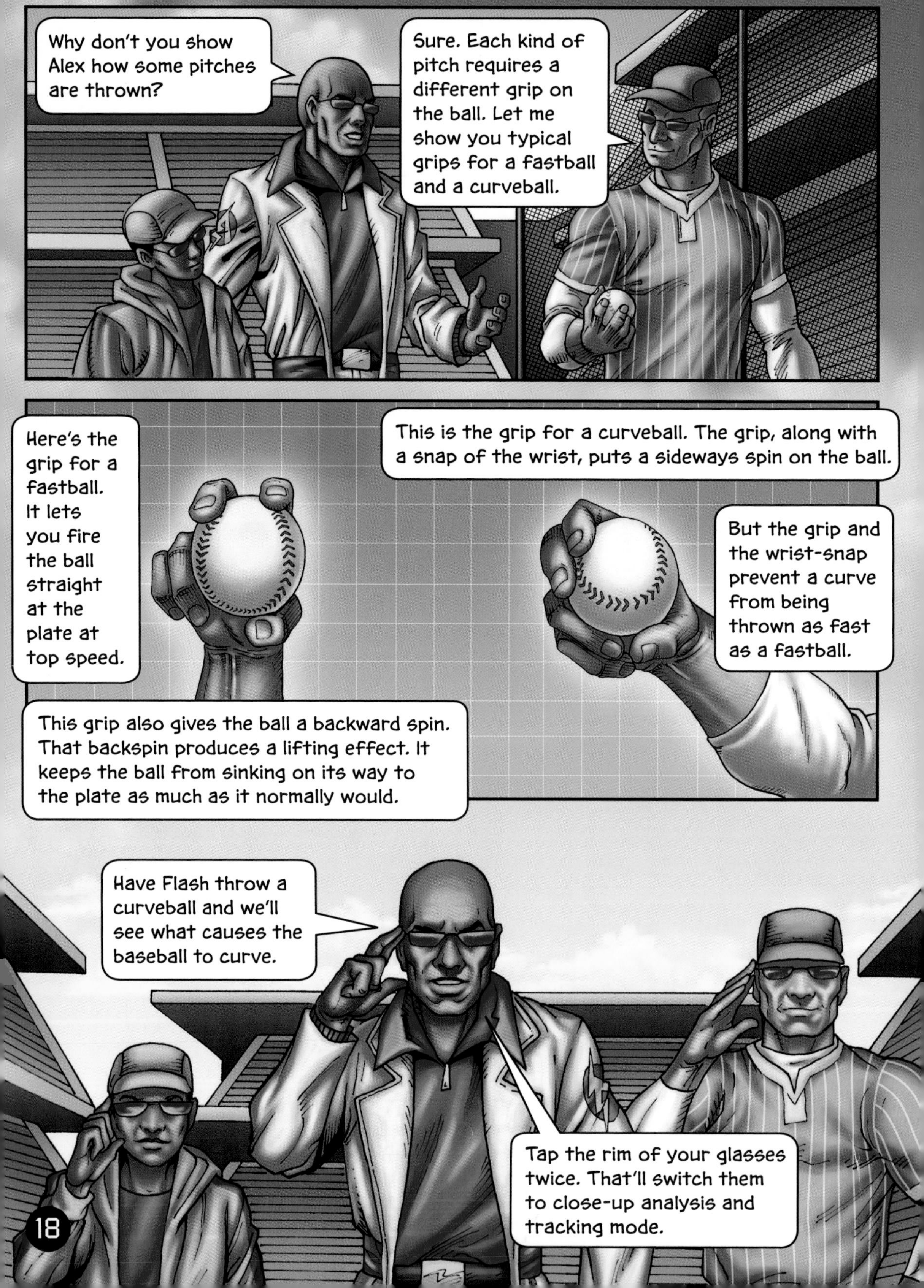
Why don't you show Alex how some pitches are thrown?
Sure. Each kind of pitch requires a different grip on the ball. Let me show you typical grips for a fastball and a curveball.
Here's the grip for a fastball. It lets you fire the ball straight at the plate at top speed.
This is the grip for a curveball. The grip, along with a snap of the wrist, puts a sideways spin on the ball.
But the grip and the wrist-snap prevent a curve from being thrown as fast as a fastball.
This grip also gives the ball a backward spin. That backspin produces a lifting effect. It keeps the ball from sinking on its way to the plate as much as it normally would.
Have Flash throw a curveball and we'll see what causes the baseball to curve.
Tap the rim of your glasses twice. That'll switch them to close-up analysis and tracking mode.

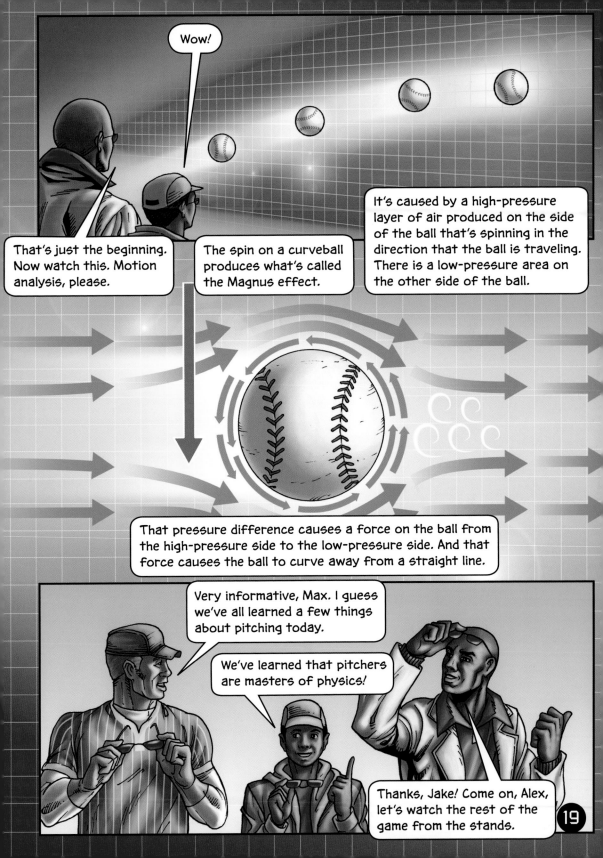

This guy slams a lot of line drives to the left side of the field.

Just like I told you!

THWACK!

WHAP!

Okay! Three up, three down!

Why did the shortstop pull his hands to his chest when he caught the ball?

That ball was moving about 110 miles an hour. The backward motion of the fielder's hands gave the ball more time to get from full speed to full stop.

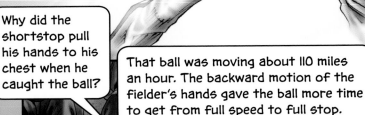

Baseball gloves changed throughout the 1900s. Every improvement in them made life easier for fielders. Padding provided force-reducing cushioning from fast-moving balls. Webbing between the thumb and index finger allowed fielders to snag balls without the ball smacking into their palms.

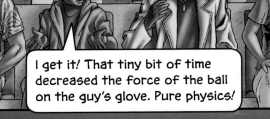

I get it! That tiny bit of time decreased the force of the ball on the guy's glove. Pure physics!

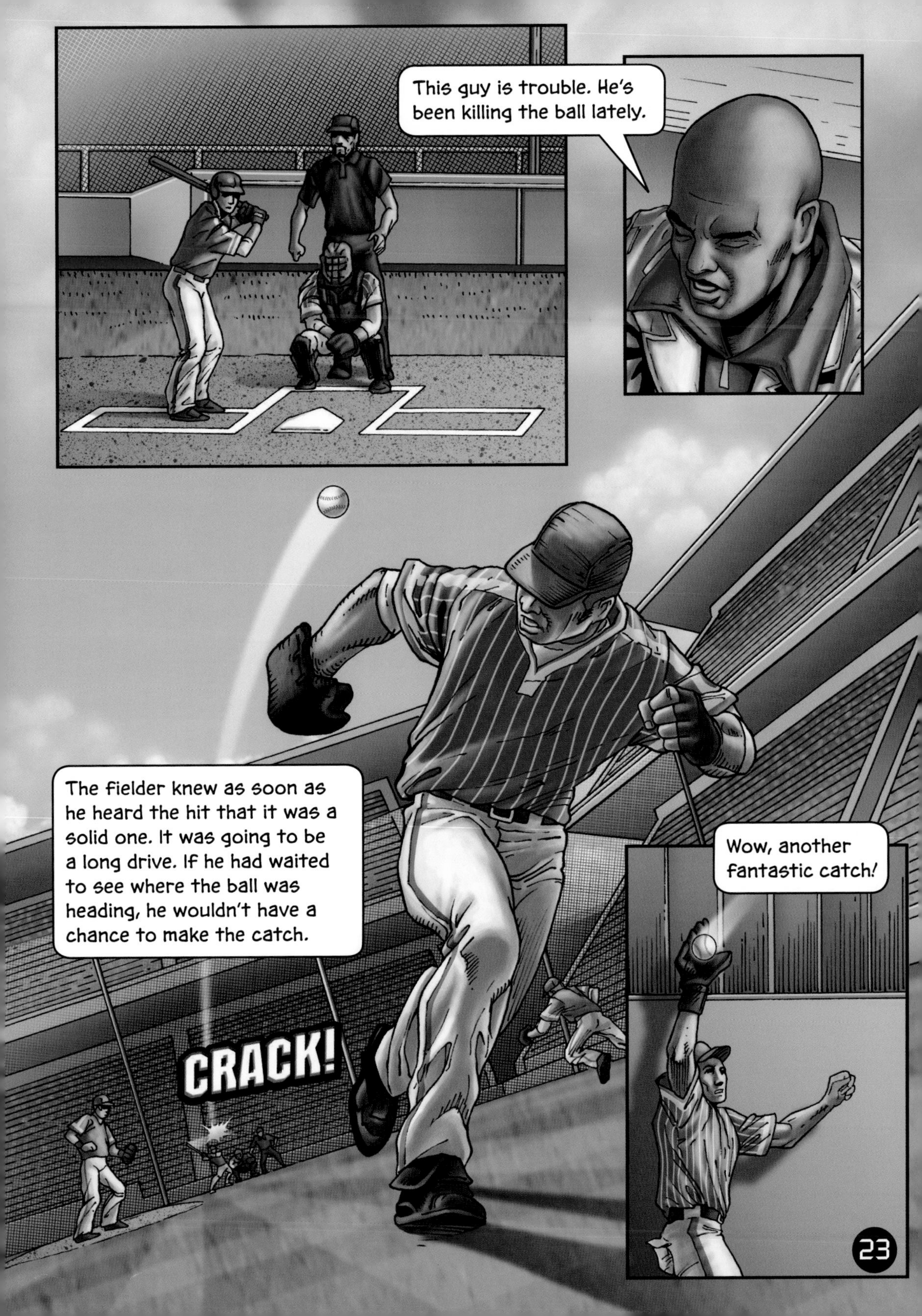
This guy is trouble. He's been killing the ball lately.
The fielder knew as soon as he heard the hit that it was a solid one. It was going to be a long drive. If he had waited to see where the ball was heading, he wouldn't have a chance to make the catch.
CRACK!
Wow, another fantastic catch!

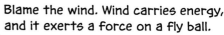

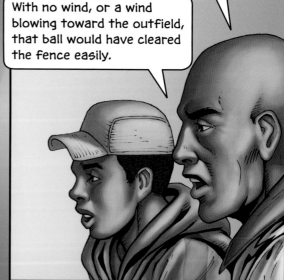

MORE ABOUT
BASEBALL

The cork-centered baseball became standard in the major leagues in 1911. This ball was livelier than the ones that had been used previously and could thus be hit farther.

One of the hardest pitches to hit—or catch—is the knuckleball. This pitch is thrown so that it rotates very slowly. Air currents moving across the seams of the ball cause it to move inconsistently. A knuckleball is said to "flutter" or "dance" on its way to the plate.

Many pitchers suffer from repetitive-stress injuries to the soft tissues of the elbow and shoulder. One of the worst stress-related injuries to a pitcher's shoulder is called a labrum tear. The labrum is a layer of cartilage that, with ligaments, keeps the upper arm bone properly connected to the shoulder. A torn labrum requires surgery, which often is not completely successful. A labrum tear can end a pitcher's career.

Batters often insist that a fastball rises or "hops" a few inches when nearing the plate. But physicists explain that a baseball cannot rise on its way to the plate. All overhand pitches drop continually from the force of gravity. But if a pitch comes to the plate faster than a batter expects, it will drop less than he anticipates. That difference in height makes the ball appear to rise.

For most of baseball's history, the only way to measure the distance of a home run hit out of a park was with a tape measure. In recent years, however, special cameras and computer programs have made it possible to measure long hits electronically. These systems can also determine how far a home run that hits an obstacle would have traveled.

MORE ABOUT

MAX AXIOM

SUPER SCIENTIST

Real name: Maxwell J. Axiom
Hometown: Seattle, Washington
Height: 6' 1" Weight: 192 lbs
Eyes: Brown Hair: None

Super capabilities: Super intelligence; able to shrink to the size of an atom; sunglasses give x-ray vision; lab coat allows for travel through time and space.

Origin: Since birth, Max Axiom seemed destined for greatness. His mother, a marine biologist, taught her son about the mysteries of the sea. His father, a nuclear physicist and volunteer park ranger, schooled Max on the wonders of earth and sky.

One day on a wilderness hike, a megacharged lightning bolt struck Max with blinding fury. When he awoke, Max discovered a newfound energy and set out to learn as much about science as possible. He traveled the globe earning degrees in every aspect of the field. Upon his return, he was ready to share his knowledge and new identity with the world. He had become Max Axiom, Super Scientist.

GLOSSARY

center of mass (SEN-tur UV MASS)—the point around which all of an object's mass, or weight, is evenly distributed

crow hop (KRO HOPP)—a series of motions an outfielder uses to generate force in his body and transfer it to the baseball for a long throw

energy (EH-ner-jee)—the ability to do work

force (FORS)—an act that changes the movement of an object

inertia (ih-NER-shuh)—tendency of an object to remain either at rest or in motion unless affected by an outside force

lever (LEH-ver)—a tool that multiplies or changes the direction of an applied force; a crowbar is an example of a lever

Magnus effect (MAG-nuhs uh-FEKT)—a force produced by differences in air pressure around a spinning object

moment of inertia (MOH-ment UV ih-NER-shuh)—a measure of how hard it is to change the speed of an object rotating around a pivot point; a bat with a high moment of inertia is harder to swing than a bat with a low moment of inertia

momentum (moh-MEN-tum)—the amount of force in a moving object determined by the object's mass and speed

pivot point (PIH-vut POYNT)—a point about six inches above the knob of a bat around which the bat is swung

sweet spot (SWEET SPOT)—the place on a bat where a hit is most solid and produces the least amount of vibration

swing weight (SWING WATE)—the "feel" of a bat in a batter's hands; bats of the same actual weight can have different swing weights depending on how their mass is distributed

READ MORE

Adamson, Thomas K. *Baseball: the Math of the Game.* Sports Illustrated KIDS. Mankato, Minn.: Capstone Sports, 2012.

Dreier, David L. *Baseball: How It Works.* The Science of Sports. Mankato, Minn.: Capstone Press, 2010.

Graubart, Norman D. *The Science of Baseball.* Sports Science. New York: PowerKids Press, 2016.

Hetrick, Hans. *Play Baseball Like a Pro: Key Skills and Tips.* Play Like the Pros. Mankato, Minn.: Capstone Press, 2011.

INTERNET SITES

FactHound offers a safe, fun way to find Internet sites related to this book. All sites on FactHound have been researched by our staff.

Here's all you do:

Visit www.facthound.com

Type in this code: 9781491460832

Check out projects, games and lots more at
www.capstonekids.com

INDEX